The Amazingly boring book of...

DULL FACTS

UK Edition

CONTENTS

Food
and
Drink

Top cheese consumers
(Pounds Per Capita Per Year)

1.   France: 57.9
2.   Germany: 53.2
3.   Luxembourg: 53.2
4.   Iceland: 53.2
5.   Greece: 51.5
6.   Finland: 49.5
7.   Italy: 48.0
8.   Switzerland: 48
9.   Estonia: 45.8
10.   Netherlands: 42.7

Fisherman's Friend

Developed in 1865 by the
pharmacist, James Lofthouse

Designed to relieve respiratory
problems experienced by sailors

Margaret Thatcher was a fan
of them and so is Emmanuel
Macron!

Available in 20
different flavours, such as:

Lemon
Mint
Blackcurrant
Apple
Mint Choc
Grapefruit
Cherry

Founded in Fleetwood, Lancashire
and produced there ever since.

5 billion lozenges produced
every year!

Did you know?

One biscuit has, on average,
about 166 calories.

A calorie is is technically defined as the
amount of energy needed to raise the
temperature of 1 gram of water by 1
degree Celsius.

There are over 5000 different
varieties of potato.

The thickness of sliced bread varies
around the world. It can be anything
from 12-24mm, with standard being
around 14mm.
(see chart)

SLICE COUNT	NAME	THICKNESS	Slice Weight
22+2 crusts	Medium	9.5mm +/- 2mm	15g +/- 3g
16+2 crusts	Thick	12.5mm +/- 2mm	22g +/- 3g
14+2 crusts	SXL	14mm +/- 2mm	24g +/- 3g
12+2 crusts	Extra thick	16mm +/- 2mm	27g +/- 3g
11+2 crusts	Doorstep	17mm +/- 2mm	29g +/- 3g

A kettle takes between two
to four minutes to boil water.

The word Spam comes from
spiced pork and ham.

A jar of ground spice such as
cumin, paprika, ginger
or chilli powder has a shelf life
of about 2 - 4 years.

Milk lid colours around the world

AUSTRALIA

Blue top - Regular milk
Purple top - Reduced Fat milk
Light blue top - Low Fat milk
Red top - Skim milk
Gold Top - Unhomogenized

CANADA

Blue top - Skim milk or 2% milk
Purple top - 1% milk
Pink top - 2% milk
Green top - 1% milk
Red top - 3.8% or homogenized milk
White - chocolate milk
Yellow top - Homogenized milk or skim milk
Brown - Chocolate milk

PEOPLE'S REPUBLIC OF CHINA

Blue top - Whole Milk
Red - Reduced Fat
Dark Green - Low Fat
Light Green - Skim

HONG KONG

Silver top - 3.5g fat and 110mg Calcium
Green top - hi-calcium with 2.0g fat and
165mg of Calcium
Gold top - slim milk with 2g fat and
160mg calcium or milk full cream with
milk re-added

DENMARK

Purple - Skim milk
Light blue - 2% milk
Dark Green - Whole milk
Light Green - Unpasteurized
Butterscotch - Half and Half

FINLAND

Red - whole milk (3.5% fat)
Dark blue - normal milk (1.5% fat)
Blue - light milk (1% fat)
Light blue - fat free milk

FRANCE

Aluminum top - Skim milk
Red top - whole milk
Blue top - 1% milk
Yellow top - 2% milk
Green top - cream

GERMANY

Lavender top - Skim milk
Light blue top - 1% milk
Dark Blue top - 2% milk
Green top - Whole Milk
Light Green top -Buttermilk
Brown top - Chocolate Milk

ISRAEL

Red top - Kefir
Blue top - Whole milk
Light blue top - 2% milk
Green top - 1% milk
Light green - Skim milk

RUSSIA

Green top - Whole Milk
Blue top - Half Milk
Red top - Reduced Milk
Pink top - Low fat
Yellow top - Skim Milk

UNITED STATES

Red top - Whole Milk.
Pink or light blue top - Skim Milk.
Blue top - 2% milk.
Yellow or purple top - 1% milk.
Brown top - chocolate milk.
Green top - buttermilk.
White top - Unhomogenized milk.
Black top - Unpasteurized milk.

Home and Garden

Did you know?

LAWNMOWERS

The lawnmower was invented in 1830!

North America had a 35.03% market share of sales in 2022!

The average garden size in Great Britain is 188 square metres!

Grass typically grows about 2 to 3cm per week!

Grass Green is 15-6437 TCX
on a Pantone colour chart

Southport in Merseyside is
home to the British
Lawnmower Museum, which
has a collection of over 300
mowers.

Around the world, there are
11,400 known grasses.

INSIDE A

BRITISH

3 PIN PLUG

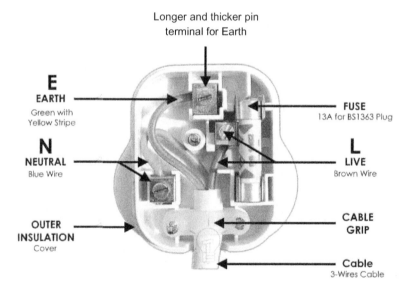

Longer and thicker pin
terminal for Earth

E
EARTH
Green with
Yellow Stripe

FUSE
13A for BS1363 Plug

N
NEUTRAL
Blue Wire

L
LIVE
Brown Wire

**OUTER
INSULATION**
Cover

**CABLE
GRIP**

Cable
3-Wires Cable

SOCKS

It comes from the Latin word 'soccus',
meaning a loose-fitting slipper worn by
Roman comedy actors on stage.

Your feet can sweat up to half
a litre a day!

The oldest known pair of socks is
1,600 years old

A design on the ankle or side of a
sock is called a clock

Datang, China is known as "Sock City"
and is the world's top annual
sock producer, manufacturing 40%
of socks globally every year.

DUST

Over the course of a week, the average person generates around a third of an ounce of dead skin. To put this into context, that's the same weight as a car key.

Most of the dust in the atmosphere comes from the Sahara Desert.

Scientists estimate that the average home generates around 40 pounds of dust every year.

During the infamous Dust Bowl event of the 1930s, thousands of Americans succumbed to dust pneumonia.

TOG rating

The tog is a measure of thermal insulance of a unit area

The Shirley Institute in Manchester, England developed the tog as an easy-to-follow guide to warmth

Duvets come in TOG ratings between 3 and 15.

Thermal socks have a tog rating of about 2.3

Tog Values of Duvets versus Temperature

Air Temp. Centigrade	Summer 3 - 4.5 tog	Spring-Autumn 7.5 - 10.5 tog	Winter 12 - 13.5 tog
24			
23			
22			
21			
20			
19			
18			
17			
16			
15			
14			
13			
12			
11			
10			
9			
8			

THREAD COUNT

The thread count of a fabric refers to the number of threads woven per square inch. This figure is used to determine the quality of a fabric item, with luxury textiles tending to have a much higher thread count than others.

Starting at around 60, thread counts can reach figures as high as 800 and over.

Good quality sheets start at 180 thread count.

Common
screw heads

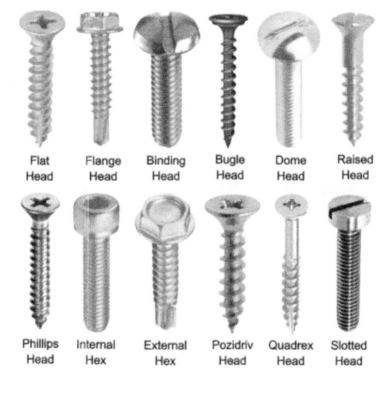

| Flat Head | Flange Head | Binding Head | Bugle Head | Dome Head | Raised Head |

| Phillips Head | Internal Hex | External Hex | Pozidriv Head | Quadrex Head | Slotted Head |

Sport

TEAMS THAT FINISHED SECOND

FIFA World Cups

1930 - Argentina

1934 - Czechoslovakia

1938 - Hungary

1950 - Brazil

1954 - Hungary

1958 - Sweden

1962 - Czechoslovakia

1966 - West Germany

1970 - Italy

1974 - Netherlands

1978 - Netherlands

1982 - West Germany

1986 - West Germany

1990 - Argentina

1994 - Italy

1998 - Brazil

2002 - Germany

2006 - France

2010 - Netherlands

2014 - Argentina

2018 - Croatia

2022 - France

Did you know?

Garry Kasparov is one of the most successful World Chess champions ever.

He has won six titles between the years 1985 and 1995.

Kasparov was ranked world no. 1 for a record 255 months overall.

Kasparov became the youngest-ever undisputed world champion aged 22

He has size 9 feet.

Transport
and
Motoring

———————□

TRAFFIC CONES FUN FACTS

There are about 140 million
traffic cones in use worldwide

Rubber traffic cones have been
mass produced since 1947

They first graced a stretch
of the then M1, the UK's first
motorway, that went
past Preston.

Traffic cone colours and what they mean

Orange

This is the standard colour for a road cone. You'll see these mostly on roads and around work/construction sites. They either signify a hazard or are commonly used for parking control.

Yellow and white

This colour cone indicates that you aren't allowed to stop or wait in this area.

Blue and white

If you see this colour traffic cone, it
means that there's a possible risk
overhead to be aware of,
such as power lines.

Green and white

You'll often see these on motorways
when there are roadworks. They indicate
an opening to access lanes.

Red

Everyone knows red means danger.
You'll see these cones in areas where
there's a hazard that could cause
injury or even death.

BUSES

There are around 3 billion journeys
made on local buses in England
every year

31,00 buses are used by local operators.
9,000 of these are are London.

19% of them had charging points
in 2022

Most local bus services in the UK are
run by 5 large companies – the Big 5.
They are:
Arriva UK
Go-Ahead Group
FirstGroup
National Express
Stagecoach Group

There are 13 tax bands for cars registered after 1st April 2017.

The most expensive costs £2605 a year!

As of 2018, the Lamborghini Aventador has the highest level of CO_2 emissions at 370 g/km

Average price of cars that pay the highest first year VED rate is £160,307

VED stands for Vehicle Excise Duty

The numbers found on oil refer to the viscosity. In the oil grade 5w 3o the 5 refers to the viscosity in cold weather (with the w standing for winter) and the 30 refers to oil flow at higher temperatures.

the minimum legal tread depth is 1.6mm across the middle three quarters of the tyre.

56 miles per hours is considered to be the most economical speed for motorway driving.

An average family car has around 300 litres of boot space.

RING ROADS

The idea of orbital "ring roads" around London actually got its start in 1937.

London has three ring roads (the M25 motorway, the North and South Circular roads and the Inner Ring Road).

Birmingham also has three ring roads which consist of the Birmingham Box; the A4540, commonly known as the Middleway; and the A4040, the Outer Ring Road. Birmingham once had a fourth ring road, the A4400.

SERVICE STATIONS

There are 105 motorway service stations in the UK.

Newport Pagnell and Watford Gap were the first stations to open in 1960.

The first alphabetically is Abingdon in South Lanarkshire, operated by Welcome Break on the M74.

There are no service stations beginning with the letters I, J, Q, U, V, X, Y or Z.

In a 2022 survey, Rugby Services, on the M6, was named the UK's best motorway service station.

THE HIGHWAY CODE

Originally published in 1931.

In 2022 the 17th edition
was issued.

The first issue cost one pence.

Leslie Hore-Belisha's 1934 Road
Traffic Act introduced a 30mph speed
limit in built-up areas

It also brought in stronger
penalties for reckless driving
and required cyclists
to have rear reflectors.

MOTORWAYS

There are 50 motorways in
Great Britain with over 8,300 km of
roads and 666 junctions

The A8(M) is the UK's shortest
motorway, running for just over 280
metres (308 yards). It forms a link
between two roundabouts at Baillieston
Interchange, better known as the
junction between the M8 and M73.

At 231 miles (370km), **the M6** is the
UK's longest motorway. It runs from
Catthorpe (junction 19 on the M1) to the
Scottish Border.

The M62 is the highest motorway in the UK. It reaches 1,220ft (372m) near the Pennine Way footbridge.

The M25 is the busiest motorway, used by about 200,000 cars every day.

CAT'S EYE COLOURS

Red studs warn motorists that they are close to the left edge of the road.

Amber studs warn drivers of the central reservation of a dual carriageway or motorway.

Green studs signify the edge of the main carriageway where rest-areas and access roads exit the main road.

Most popular colours of car

- GREY: 25.7% - accounting for 415,199 new cars sold.
- BLACK: 20.1% - accounting for 324,993 new cars sold.
- WHITE: 16.7% - accounting for 268,886 new cars sold.
- BLUE: 16% - accounting for 259,950 new cars sold.
- RED: 8.5% - accounting for 136,793 new cars sold.

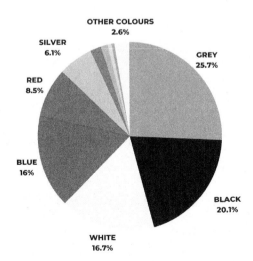

OTHER COLOURS 2.6%
SILVER 6.1%
RED 8.5%
BLUE 16%
WHITE 16.7%
BLACK 20.1%
GREY 25.7%

ROADS (General)

A pothole will be identified when it has a maximum horizontal dimension greater than 75mm and a depth greater than 20mm

The UK has about 262,000 miles of paved roads in total.

A manhole covers are usually made from cast iron and weigh about 113 kg.

The second most boring road in the UK is the A30 in Devon and Cornwall

PLANES

The maximum take off weight
of a Boeing 747 is 433 tons
and has 140 miles of wiring.

The fuel efficiency of a full 747
works out to about 100 miles
per gallon per person.

Dutch airline KLM has the longest
continuous operating record of any
airline in the world. The Amsterdam-
based airline's planes have been lifting
off and touching down since 1919.

Airplane tires are inflated to about six
times the PSI of car tyres - about
200 pounds per square inch.

Miscellaneous

There are 76 cities in the UK.
In alphabetical order they are:

ENGLAND

Bath
Birmingham
Bradford
Brighton & Hove
Bristol
Cambridge
Canterbury
Carlisle
Chelmsford
Chester
Chichester
Colchester
Coventry
Derby
Doncaster
Durham
Ely
Exeter
Gloucester
Hereford
Kingston-upon-Hull

Lancaster
Leeds
Leicester
Lichfield
Lincoln
Liverpool
London
Manchester
Milton Keynes
Newcastle-upon-Tyne
Norwich
Nottingham
Oxford
Peterborough
Plymouth
Portsmouth
Preston
Ripon
Salford
Salisbury
Sheffield
Southampton
Southend-on-Sea
St Albans
Stoke on Trent

Sunderland
Truro
Wakefield
Wells
Westminster
Winchester
Wolverhampton
Worcester
York

NORTHERN IRELAND

Armagh
Bangor
Belfast
Lisburn
Londonderry
Newry

SCOTLAND

Aberdeen
Dundee
Dunfermline
Edinburgh
Glasgow
Inverness
Perth
Stirling

WALES

Bangor
Cardiff
Newport
St Asaph
St Davids
Swansea
Wrexham

BEIGE

Beige is variously described as a pale sandy fawn color, a grayish tan, a light-grayish yellowish brown, or a pale to grayish yellow.

It takes its name from French, where the word originally meant natural wool that has been neither bleached nor dyed, hence also the color of natural wool.

Beige began to commonly be used as a term for a colour in France beginning approximately 1855–60.

Beige is notoriously difficult to produce in traditional offset CMYK printing

Did you know?

SKIPS

- Skips come in many different sizes. Small ones hold about 2-3 cubic yards of waste while larger skips can hold up to 12 cubic yards of waste.

- On Average small skips cost around £100 to £300, whereas larger ones cost about £250 to £500.

GMC Imperial - Metric Conversion Table

2mm ($5/64$ in)	60mm (2 $3/8$ in)	210mm (8 ¼ in)	840mm (33 in)
3mm ($1/8$ in)	63mm (2 ½ in)	215mm (8 ½ in)	865mm (34 in)
4mm ($5/32$ in)	65mm (2 $5/8$ in)	220mm (8 $3/4$ in)	890mm (35 in)
6mm (¼ in)	70mm (2 $3/4$ in)	230mm (9 in)	915mm (36 in)
7mm ($9/32$ in)	75mm (3 in)	235mm (9 ¼ in)	940mm (37 in)
8mm ($5/16$ in)	80mm (3 $1/8$ in)	240mm (9 ½ in)	965mm (38 in)
9mm ($11/32$ in)	85mm (3 ¼ in)	250mm (9 $3/4$ in)	990mm (39 in)
10mm ($3/8$ in)	90mm (3 ½ in)	255mm (10 in)	1015mm (40 in)
11mm ($7/16$ in)	93mm (3 $2/3$ in)	257mm (10 $1/8$ in)	1040mm (41 in)
12mm (½ in)	95mm (3 $3/4$ in)	280mm (11 in)	1065mm (42 in)
13mm (½ in)	100mm (4 in)	305mm (12 in)	1090mm (43 in)
14mm ($9/16$ in)	105mm (4 $1/8$ in)	330mm (13 in)	1120mm (44 in)
15mm ($9/16$ in)	110mm (4 ¼ - 4 $3/8$ in)	355mm (14 in)	1145mm (45 in)
16mm ($5/8$ in)	115mm (4 ½ in)	380mm (15 in)	1170mm (46 in)
17mm ($11/16$ in)	120mm (4 $3/4$ in)	405mm (16 in)	1195mm (47 in)
18mm ($23/32$ in)	125mm (5 in)	430mm (17 in)	1220mm (48 in)
19mm ($3/4$ in)	130mm (5 $1/8$ in)	460mm (18 in)	1245mm (49 in)
20mm ($3/4$ in)	135mm (5 ¼ in)	485mm (19 in)	1270mm (50 in)
21mm ($13/16$ in)	140mm (5 ½ in)	510mm (20 in)	1295mm (51 in)
22mm ($7/8$ in)	145mm (5 $3/4$ in)	535mm (21 in)	1320mm (52 in)
23mm ($29/32$ in)	150mm (6 in)	560mm (22 in)	1345mm (53 in)
24mm ($15/16$ in)	155mm (6 $1/8$ in)	585mm (23 in)	1370mm (54 in)
25mm (1 in)	160mm (6 ¼ in)	610mm (24 in)	1395mm (55 in)
30mm (1 $1/8$ in)	165mm (6 ½ in)	635mm (25 in)	1420mm (56 in)
32mm (1 ¼ in)	170mm (6 $3/4$ in)	660mm (26 in)	1450mm (57 in)
35mm (1 $3/8$ in)	178mm (6 $7/8$ in)	685mm (27 in)	1475mm (58 in)
38mm (1 ½ in)	180mm (7 in)	710mm (28 in)	1500mm (59 in)
40mm (1 $5/8$ in)	185mm (7 ¼ in)	735mm (29 in)	1525mm (60 in)
45mm (1 $3/4$ in)	190mm (7 ½ in)	760mm (30 in)	
50mm (2 in)	195mm (7 $3/4$ in)	785mm (31 in)	
55mm (2 $1/8$ - 2 ¼ in)	200mm (8 in)	815mm (32 in)	

Know your acronyms

PIN - stands for Personal Identification number, so if you say 'PIN number' then you are actually saying 'Personal Identification Number Number'.

LASER - **L**ight **A**mplification by **S**timulated **E**mission of **R**adiation

QANTAS - Queensland and Northern Territory Aerial Services

SCUBA - Self-Contained Underwater Breathing Apparatus

PVC - Polyvinyl Chloride

DNA - Deoxyribonucleic Acid

LDPE - Low-density polyethylene

HDPE - High-density polyethylene

HTTP - Hypertext Transfer Protocol

PSI - Pounds per square inch

GSM - Grams per square metre

Did you know?

ABA is an acronym for 7
different organisations!

Adriatic Basketball Association

American Bar Association

American Basketball Association

American Beverage Association

American Bicycle Association

American Birding Association

Australian Broadcasting Authority

TOILETS AND SEWERAGE

A standard toilet uses about
7 litres of water per flush

In a survey the cleanest public
toilets in the world were found
in Singapore.

The cleanest loos in the UK
are found in Leeds and the
least hygienic in Peterborough.

99% of public toilets in
Edinburgh are free to use.

Beckton Sewage Works is
the largest water treatment
centre in the UK.

COMMONLY USED WORDS THAT ARE ACTUALLY BRANDS

Portakabin - Portable building

Post it note - sticky note

Sellotape - Sticky tape

Portaloo - Portable toilet

Tupperware - plastic food storage boxes

Velcro - Hook and loop fastener

Astroturf - Artificial grass

ROOF TRUSSES

There are many different types of
roof truss:

Common
Gable
Dual Ridge
Scissor
Mono
King Post
Queen Post
Fan
Fink
Howe
Raised tie
Double pitch profile
and more...

THE HUMAN BODY

The average person yawns 7.5
times per day.

The bladder can hold about
500ml of urine, but most
people need to visit the toilet
when it's about half full.

Fingernails grow about 3mm
per month.

The feet each have 250,000 sweat glands
– only the scalp and armpits can secrete
more sweat than the feet. Furthermore,
the feet can carry more than 100,000
different types of bacteria – some
healthy, some not.

DIALLING CODES

Area codes were introduced back in 1958 when callers were, for the first time, able to call another telephone number directly instead of via a manual telephone exchange operator. Over the next 20 years uniform exchange codes (STD codes) were allocated to every exchange in the country until completion in 1979.
Here they are, in all their glory:

0113 Leeds
0114 Sheffield
0115 Nottingham
0116 Leicester
0117 Bristol
0118 Reading
01200 Clitheroe
01202 Bournemouth
01204 Bolton
01205 Boston
01206 Colchester
01207 Consett
01208 Bodmin
01209 Redruth
0121 Birmingham

01223 Cambridge
01224 Aberdeen
01225 Bath
01226 Barnsley
01227 Canterbury
01228 Carlisle
01229 Barrow-in Furness / Millom
01233 Ashford (Kent)
01234 Bedford
01235 Abingdon
01236 Coatbridge
01237 Bideford
01239 Cardigan
01241 Arbroath
01242 Cheltenham
01243 Chichester
01244 Chester
01245 Chelmsford
01246 Chesterfield
01248 Bangor (Gwynedd)
01249 Chippenham
01250 Blairgowrie
01252 Aldershot
01253 Blackpool
01254 Blackburn
01255 Clacton-on-Sea
01256 Basingstoke
01257 Coppull

01258 Blandford
01259 Alloa
01260 Congleton
01261 Banff
01262 Bridlington
01263 Cromer
01264 Andover
01267 Carmarthen
01268 Basildon
01269 Ammanford
01270 Crewe
01271 Barnstaple
01273 Brighton
01274 Bradford
01275 Clevedon
01276 Camberley
01277 Brentwood
01278 Bridgwater
01279 Bishops Stortford
01280 Buckingham
01282 Burnley
01283 Burton-on-Trent
01284 Bury-St-Edmunds
01285 Cirencester
01286 Caernarvon
01287 Guisborough
01288 Bude
01289 Berwick-on-Tweed

01290 Cumnock
01291 Chepstow
01292 Ayr
01293 Crawley
01294 Ardrossan
01295 Banbury
01296 Aylesbury
01297 Axminster
01298 Buxton
01299 Bewdley
01300 Cerne Abbas
01301 Arrochar
01302 Doncaster
01303 Folkestone
01304 Dover
01305 Dorchester
01306 Dorking
01307 Forfar
01308 Bridport
01309 Forres
0131 Edinburgh
01320 Fort Augustus
01322 Dartford
01323 Eastbourne
01324 Falkirk
01325 Darlington
01326 Falmouth
01327 Daventry

01328 Fakenham
01329 Fareham
01330 Banchory
01332 Derby
01333 Peat Inn
01334 St Andrews
01335 Ashbourne
01337 Ladybank
01339 Aboyne / Ballater
01340 Craigellachie
01341 Barmouth
01342 East Grinstead
01343 Elgin
01344 Bracknell
01346 Fraserburgh
01347 Easingwold
01348 Fishguard
01349 Dingwall
01350 Dunkeld
01352 Mold
01353 Ely
01354 Chatteris
01355 East Kilbride
01356 Brechin
01357 Strathaven
01358 Ellon
01359 Pakenham
01360 Killearn
01361 Duns

01362 Dereham
01363 Crediton
01364 Ashburton
01366 Downham Market
01367 Faringdon
01368 Dunbar
01369 Dunoon
01371 Great Dunmow
01372 Esher
01373 Frome
01375 Grays Thurrock
01376 Braintree
01377 Driffield
01379 Diss
01380 Devizes
01381 Fortrose
01382 Dundee
01383 Dunfermline
01384 Dudley
01386 Evesham
01387 Dumfries
013873 Langholm
01388 Bishop Auckland / Stanhope
01389 Dumbarton
01392 Exeter
01394 Felixstowe
01395 Budleigh Salterton
01397 Fort William
01398 Dulverton

01400 Honington
01403 Horsham
01404 Honiton
01405 Goole
01406 Holbeach
01407 Holyhead
01408 Golspie
01409 Holsworthy
0141 Glasgow
01420 Alton
01422 Halifax
01423 Boroughbridge / Harrogate
01424 Hastings
01425 Ringwood
01427 Gainsborough
01428 Haslemere
01429 Hartlepool
01430 Market Weighton / North Cave
01431 Helmsdale
01432 Hereford
01433 Hathersage
01434 Bellingham / Haltwhistle / Hexham
01435 Heathfield
01436 Helensburgh
01437 Clynderwen / Haverfordwest
01438 Stevenage
01439 Helmsley
01440 Haverhill
01442 Hemel Hempstead

01443 Pontypridd
01444 Haywards Heath
01445 Gairloch
01446 Barry
01449 Stowmarket
01450 Hawick
01451 Stow-on-the-Wold
01452 Gloucester
01453 Dursley
01454 Chipping Sodbury
01455 Hinckley
01456 Glenurquhart
01457 Glossop
01458 Glastonbury
01460 Chard
01461 Gretna
01462 Hitchin
01463 Inverness
01464 Insch
01465 Girvan
01466 Huntly
01467 Inverurie
01469 Killingholme
01470 Isle of Skye - Edinbane
01471 Isle of Skye - Broadford
01472 Grimsby
01473 Ipswich
01474 Gravesend
01475 Greenock

01476 Grantham
01477 Holmes Chapel
01478 Isle of Skye - Portree
01479 Grantown-on-Spey
01480 Huntingdon
01481 Guernsey
01482 Hull
01483 Guildford
01484 Huddersfield
01485 Hunstanton
01487 Warboys
01488 Hungerford
01489 Bishops Waltham
01490 Corwen
01491 Henley-on-Thames
01492 Colwyn Bay
01493 Great Yarmouth
01494 High Wycombe
01495 Pontypool
01496 Port Ellen
01497 Hay-on-Wye
01499 Inveraray
01501 Harthill
01502 Lowestoft
01503 Looe
01505 Johnstone
01506 Bathgate
01507 Alford (Lincs) / Louth / Spilsby
01508 Brooke

01509 Loughborough
0151 Liverpool
01520 Lochcarron
01522 Lincoln
01524 Lancaster
015242 Hornby
01525 Leighton Buzzard
01526 Martin
01527 Redditch
01528 Laggan
01529 Sleaford
01530 Coalville
01531 Ledbury
01534 Jersey
01535 Keighley
01536 Kettering
01538 Ipstones
01539 Kendal
015394 Hawkshead
015395 Grange-Over-Sands
015396 Sedbergh
01540 Kingussie
01542 Keith
01543 Cannock
01544 Kington
01545 Llanarth
01546 Lochgilphead
01547 Knighton
01548 Kingsbridge

01549 Lairg
01550 Llandovery
01553 Kings Lynn
01554 Llanelli
01555 Lanark
01556 Castle Douglas
01557 Kirkcudbright
01558 Llandeilo
01559 Llandysul
01560 Moscow
01561 Laurencekirk
01562 Kidderminster
01563 Kilmarnock
01564 Lapworth
01565 Knutsford
01566 Launceston
01567 Killin
01568 Leominster
01569 Stonehaven
01570 Lampeter
01571 Lochinver
01572 Oakham
01573 Kelso
01575 Kirriemuir
01576 Lockerbie
01577 Kinross
01578 Lauder
01579 Liskeard
01580 Cranbrook

01581 New Luce
01582 Luton
01583 Carradale
01584 Ludlow
01586 Campbeltown
01588 Bishops Castle
01590 Lymington
01591 Llanwrtyd Wells
01592 Kirkcaldy
01593 Lybster
01594 Lydney
01595 Lerwick / Foula / Fair Isle
01597 Llandrindod Wells
01598 Lynton
01599 Kyle
01600 Monmouth
01603 Norwich
01604 Northampton
01606 Northwich
01608 Chipping Norton
01609 Northallerton
0161 Manchester
01620 North Berwick
01621 Maldon
01622 Maidstone
01623 Mansfield
01624 Isle of Man
01625 Macclesfield
01626 Newton Abbot

01628 Maidenhead
01629 Matlock
01630 Market Drayton
01631 Oban
01633 Newport
01634 Medway
01635 Newbury
01636 Newark
01637 Newquay
01638 Newmarket
01639 Neath
01641 Strathy
01642 Middlesbrough
01643 Minehead
01644 New Galloway
01646 Milford Haven
01647 Moretonhampstead
01650 Cemmaes Road
01651 Oldmeldrum
01652 Brigg
01653 Malton
01654 Machynlleth
01655 Maybole
01656 Bridgend
01659 Sanquhar
01661 Prudhoe
01663 New Mills
01664 Melton Mowbray
01665 Alnwick

01666 Malmesbury
01667 Nairn
01668 Bamburgh
01669 Rothbury
01670 Morpeth
01671 Newton Stewart
01672 Marlborough
01673 Market Rasen
01674 Montrose
01675 Coleshill
01676 Meriden
01677 Bedale
01678 Bala
01680 Isle of Mull - Craignure
01681 Isle of Mull - Fionnphort
01683 Moffat
01684 Malvern
01685 Merthyr Tydfil
01686 Llanidloes / Newtown
01687 Mallaig
01688 Isle of Mull - Tobermory
01689 Orpington
01690 Betws-y-Coed
01691 Oswestry
01692 North Walsham
01694 Church Stretton
01695 Skelmersdale
01697 Brampton
016973 Wigton

016974 Raughton Head
016977 Brampton
01698 Motherwell
01700 Rothesay
01702 Southend-on-Sea
01704 Southport
01706 Rochdale
01707 Welwyn Garden City
01708 Romford
01709 Rotherham
01720 Isles of Scilly
01721 Peebles
01722 Salisbury
01723 Scarborough
01724 Scunthorpe
01725 Rockbourne
01726 St Austell
01727 St Albans
01728 Saxmundham
01729 Settle
01730 Petersfield
01732 Sevenoaks
01733 Peterborough
01736 Penzance
01737 Redhill
01738 Perth
01740 Sedgefield
01743 Shrewsbury
01744 St Helens

01745 Rhyl
01746 Bridgnorth
01747 Shaftesbury
01748 Richmond
01749 Shepton Mallet
01750 Selkirk
01751 Pickering
01752 Plymouth
01753 Slough
01754 Skegness
01756 Skipton
01757 Selby
01758 Pwllheli
01759 Pocklington
01760 Swaffham
01761 Temple Cloud
01763 Royston
01764 Crieff
01765 Ripon
01766 Porthmadog
01767 Sandy
01768 Penrith
017683 Appleby
017684 Pooley Bridge
017687 Keswick
01769 South Molton
01770 Isle of Arran
01771 Maud

01772 Preston
01773 Ripley
01775 Spalding
01776 Stranraer
01777 Retford
01778 Bourne
01779 Peterhead
01780 Stamford
01782 Stoke-on-Trent
01784 Staines
01785 Stafford
01786 Stirling
01787 Sudbury
01788 Rugby
01789 Stratford-upon-Avon
01790 Spilsby
01792 Swansea
01793 Swindon
01794 Romsey
01795 Sittingbourne
01796 Pitlochry
01797 Rye
01798 Pulborough
01799 Saffron Walden
01803 Torquay
01805 Torrington
01806 Shetland
01807 Ballindalloch
01808 Tomatin

01809 Tomdoun
01821 Kinrossie
01822 Tavistock
01823 Taunton
01824 Ruthin
01825 Uckfield
01827 Tamworth
01828 Coupar Angus
01829 Tarporley
01830 Kirkwhelpington
01832 Clopton
01833 Barnard Castle
01834 Narberth
01835 St Boswells
01837 Okehampton
01838 Dalmally
01840 Camelford
01841 Newquay
01842 Thetford
01843 Thanet
01844 Thame
01845 Thirsk
01847 Thurso / Tongue
01848 Thornhill
01851 Great Bernera / Stornoway
01852 Kilmelford
01854 Ullapool
01855 Ballachulish

01856 Orkney
01857 Sanday
01858 Market Harborough
01859 Harris
01862 Tain
01863 Ardgay
01864 Abington
01865 Oxford
01866 Kilchrenan
01869 Bicester
01870 Isle of Benbecula
01871 Castlebay
01872 _Truro_
01873 Abergavenny
01874 Brecon
01875 Tranent
01876 Lochmaddy
01877 Callander
01878 Lochboisdale
01879 Scarinish
01880 Tarbert
01882 Kinloch Rannoch
01883 Caterham
01884 Tiverton
01885 Pencombe
01886 Bromyard
01887 Aberfeldy
01888 Turriff

01889 Rugeley
01890 Ayton / Coldstream
01892 Tunbridge Wells
01895 Uxbridge
01896 Galashiels
01899 Biggar
01900 Workington
01902 Wolverhampton
01903 Worthing
01904 York
01905 Worcester
01908 Milton Keynes
01909 Worksop
0191 Tyneside / Durham / Sunderland
01920 Ware
01922 Walsall
01923 Watford
01924 Wakefield
01925 Warrington
01926 Warwick
01928 Runcorn
01929 Wareham
01931 Shap
01932 Weybridge
01933 Wellingborough
01934 Weston-Super-Mare
01935 Yeovil
01937 Wetherby

001938 Welshpool
01939 Wem
01942 Wigan
01943 Guiseley
01944 West Heslerton
01945 Wisbech
01946 Whitehaven
019467 Gosforth
01947 Whitby
01948 Whitchurch
01949 Whatton
01950 Sandwick
01951 Colonsay
01952 Telford
01953 Wymondham
01954 Madingley
01955 Wick
01957 Mid Yell
01959 Westerham
01962 Winchester
01963 Wincanton
01964 Hornsea / Patrington
01967 Strontian
01968 Penicuik
01969 Leyburn
01970 Aberystwyth
01971 Scourie
01972 Glenborrodale
01974 Llanon

01975 Alford (Aberdeen) / Strathdon
01977 Pontefract
01978 Wrexham
01980 Amesbury
01981 Wormbridge
01982 Builth Wells
01983 Isle of Wight
01984 Watchet
01985 Warminster
01986 Bungay
01987 Ebbsfleet
01988 Wigtown
01989 Ross-on-Wye
01992 Lea Valley
01993 Witney
01994 St Clears
01995 Garstang
01997 Strathpeffer
01807 Ballindalloch
01808 Tomatin
01809 Tomdoun
01821 Kinrossie
01822 Tavistock
01823 Taunton
01824 Ruthin
01825 Uckfield
01827 Tamworth
01828 Coupar Angus
01829 Tarporley

01830 Kirkwhelpington
01832 Clopton
01833 Barnard Castle
01834 Narberth
01835 St Boswells
01837 Okehampton
01838 Dalmally
01840 Camelford
01841 Newquay
01842 Thetford
01843 Thanet
01844 Thame
01845 Thirsk
01847 Thurso / Tongue
01848 Thornhill
01851 Great Bernera / Stornoway
01852 Kilmelford
01854 Ullapool
01855 Ballachulish
01856 Orkney
01857 Sanday
01858 Market Harborough
01859 Harris
01862 Tain
01863 Ardgay
01864 Abington
01865 Oxford
01866 Kilchrenan

01869 Bicester
01870 Isle of Benbecula
01871 Castlebay
01872 Truro
01873 Abergavenny
01874 Brecon
01875 Tranent
01876 Lochmaddy
01877 Callander
01878 Lochboisdale
01879 Scarinish
01880 Tarbert
01882 Kinloch Rannoch
01883 Caterham
01884 Tiverton
01885 Pencombe
01886 Bromyard
01887 Aberfeldy
01888 Turriff
01889 Rugeley
01890 Ayton / Coldstream
01892 Tunbridge Wells
01895 Uxbridge
01896 Galashiels
01899 Biggar
01900 Workington
01902 Wolverhampton
01903 Worthing

01904 York
01905 Worcester
01908 Milton Keynes
01909 Worksop
0191 Tyneside / Durham / Sunderland
01920 Ware
01922 Walsall
01923 Watford
01924 Wakefield
01925 Warrington
01926 Warwick
01928 Runcorn
01929 Wareham
01931 Shap
01932 Weybridge
01933 Wellingborough
01934 Weston-Super-Mare
01935 Yeovil
01937 Wetherby
01938 Welshpool
01939 Wem
01942 Wigan
01943 Guiseley
01944 West Heslerton
01945 Wisbech
01946 Whitehaven
019467 Gosforth
01947 Whitby
01948 Whitchurch

01949 Whatton
01950 Sandwick
01951 Colonsay
01952 Telford
01953 Wymondham
01954 Madingley
01955 Wick
01957 Mid Yell
01959 Westerham
01962 Winchester
01963 Wincanton
01964 Hornsea / Patrington
01967 Strontian
01968 Penicuik
01969 Leyburn
01970 Aberystwyth
01971 Scourie
01972 Glenborrodale
01974 Llanon
01975 Alford (Aberdeen) / Strathdon
01977 Pontefract
01978 Wrexham
01980 Amesbury
01981 Wormbridge
01982 Builth Wells
01983 Isle of Wight
01984 Watchet
01985 Warminster
01986 Bungay

01987 Ebbsfleet
01988 Wigtown
01989 Ross-on-Wye
01992 Lea Valley
01993 Witney
01994 St Clears
01995 Garstang
01997 Strathpeffer
020 London
023 Southampton / Portsmouth
024 Coventry
028 Northern Ireland
029 Cardiff